Touch of the Master

Studies on Jesus

Max Lucado

General Editor

Contents

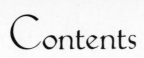

Introduction

God loves you just the way you are, but he refuses to leave you that way. He wants you to be just like Jesus.

Isn't that good news? You are changeable. You aren't stuck with today's personality. You aren't condemned to grumpy-dom. You are tweakable.

God will change you. And he will change you to be just like Jesus. Jesus felt no guilt; God wants you to feel no guilt. Jesus had no bad habits; God wants the same for you. Jesus had no anxiety about death; you needn't either. God's desire, his plan, his ultimate goal is to make you into the image of God.

As you enter this study, my prayer for you is that these pages will help you feel the Master's touch—as he touches your heart, alters your outlook, and transforms you, inside-out.

Remember, he wants you to be just like Jesus

—*Max Lucado*

Becoming Like Jesus

*"What if, for one day and one night, Jesus lives
your life with his heart? Your heart gets the day
off, and your life is led by the heart of Christ....
Would people notice a change?"—Max Lucado*

1

1. Describe a person who truly lives with the heart of
Christ.

_____

_____

_____

_____

_____

_____

_____

A Moment with Max

Max shares these insights with us in his book *Just Like Jesus*.

Where did we get the idea we can't change? From whence come statements such as, "It's just my nature to worry," or "I'll always be pessimistic. I'm just that way," or "I have a bad temper. I can't help the way I react"? Who says? Would we make similar statements about our bodies? "It's just my nature to have a broken leg. I can't do anything about it." Of course not. If our bodies malfunction, we seek help. Shouldn't we do the same with our hearts? Shouldn't we seek aid for our sour attitudes? Can't we request treatment for our selfish tirades? Of course we can. Jesus can change our hearts. He wants us to have a heart like his.

Can you imagine a better offer?
The heart of Jesus was pure....
Jesus' heart was peaceful....
His heart was purposeful....
His heart was spiritual....

2. List several excuses people give for not changing.

_____

_____

_____

_____

3. What kinds of tools does God use to make our hearts more like Jesus' heart?

_____

_____

_____

_____

A Message from the Word

[21] I know that you heard about him, and you are in him, so you were taught the truth that is in Jesus. [22] You were taught to leave your old self—to stop living the evil way you lived before. That old self becomes worse, because people are fooled by the evil things they want to do. [23] But you were taught to be made new in your hearts, [24] to become a new person. That new person is made to be like God—made to be truly good and holy.

[25] So you must stop telling lies. Tell each other the truth, because we all belong to each other in the same body. [26] When you are angry, do not sin, and be sure to stop being angry before the end of the day. [27] Do not give the devil a way to defeat you. [28] Those who are stealing must stop stealing and start working. They should earn an honest living for themselves. Then they will have something to share with those who are poor.

[29] When you talk, do not say harmful things, but say what people need—words that will help others become stronger. Then what you say will do good to those who listen to you. [30] And do not make the Holy Spirit sad. The Spirit is God's proof that you belong to him. God gave you the Spirit to show that God will make you free when the final day comes. [31] Do not be bitter or angry or mad. Never shout angrily or say things to hurt others. Never do anything evil. [32] Be kind and loving to each other, and forgive each other just as God forgave you in Christ.

[1] You are God's children whom he loves, so try to be like him. [2] Live a life of love just as Christ loved us and gave himself for us as a sweet-smelling offering and sacrifice to God.

Ephesians 4:21—5:2

4. To what extent are we able to *fix* or *change* ourselves?

_____

_____

_____

_____

_____

5. What keeps us from making necessary changes in our lives?

_____

_____

_____

_____

_____

6. List some practical benefits of living good and holy lives.

_____

_____

_____

4 _____

More from the Word

⁵ In your lives you must think and act like Christ Jesus.
⁶ Christ himself was like God in everything.
But he did not think that being equal with God was something
to be used for his own benefit.
⁷ But he gave up his place with God and made himself nothing.
He was born to be a man
and became like a servant.
⁸ And when he was living as a man,
he humbled himself and was fully obedient to God,
even when that caused his death—death on a cross.

Philippians 2:5-8

7. How do we begin thinking as Jesus does?

_____

_____

_____

_____

_____

8. What cultural pressures do we need to overcome to become servants like Jesus?

_____

_____

_____

_____

_____

_____

9. How does Christ's death on the cross enable us to change?

_____

_____

_____

_____

_____

My Reflections

"God's plan for you is nothing short of a new heart. If you were a car, God would want control of your engine. If you were a computer, God would claim the software and the hard drive. If you were an airplane, he'd take his seat in the cockpit. But you are a person, so God wants to change your heart."—Max

Journal

What is one specific change I can make in my daily routine to become more like Christ?

_____

_____

_____

_____

_____

_____

_____

_____

_____

_____

_____

7

For Further Study

To learn more about becoming like Jesus, read Romans 8:29-30; Colossians 3:10-17; Hebrews 12:2.

Additional Questions

10. What happens when we surrender our hearts to God?

_____

_____

_____

_____

_____

_____

11. How can a person determine what he or she is holding back from God?

_____

_____

_____

_____

_____

12. What motivates you to continue striving to imitate Jesus?

_____

_____

_____

_____

_____

Additional Thoughts

_____

_____

_____

_____

_____

_____

_____

_____

_____

_____

_____

Loving Difficult People

"The mercy of Christ preceded our mistakes; our mercy must precede the mistakes of others."
—*Max Lucado*

11

1. How do people typically respond when they see someone make a foolish or stupid mistake?

_____

_____

_____

_____

_____

_____

_____

_____

A Moment with Max

Max shares these insights with us in his book *Just Like Jesus*.

Jesus himself knew the feeling of being stuck with someone. For three years he ran with the same crew. By and large, he saw the same dozen or so faces around the table, around the campfire, around the clock. They rode in the same boats and walked the same roads and visited the same houses, and I wonder, how did Jesus stay so devoted to his men? Not only did he have to put up with their visible oddities, he had to endure their invisible foibles. Think about it. He could hear their unspoken thoughts. He knew their private doubts. Not only that, he knew their future doubts. What if you knew every mistake your loved ones had ever made and every mistake they would ever make? What if you knew every thought they would have about you, every irritation, every dislike, every betrayal?

Was it hard for Jesus to love Peter, knowing Peter would someday curse him? Was it tough to trust Thomas, knowing Thomas would one day question Jesus' resurrection? How did Jesus resist the urge to recruit a new batch of followers? John wanted to destroy one enemy. Peter sliced off the ear of another. Just days before Jesus' death, his disciples were arguing about which of them was the best! How was he able to love people who were hard to like?

2. Why do the very things that draw us to someone often irritate us over time?

_____

_____

_____

_____

3. In your opinion, what is the key to sustaining lifelong, committed relationships?

_____

_____

_____

A Message from the Word

[5] Then he poured water into a bowl and began to wash the followers' feet, drying them with the towel that was wrapped around him.

[6] Jesus came to Simon Peter, who said to him, "Lord, are you going to wash my feet?"

[7] Jesus answered, "You don't understand now what I am doing, but you will understand later."

[8] Peter said, "No, you will never wash my feet."

Jesus answered, "If I don't wash your feet, you are not one of my people."

[9] Simon Peter answered, "Lord, then wash not only my feet, but wash my hands and my head, too!"

[10] Jesus said, "After a person has had a bath, his whole body is clean. He needs only to wash his feet. And you men are clean, but not all of you." [11] Jesus knew who would turn against him, and that is why he said, "Not all of you are clean."

[12] When he had finished washing their feet, he put on his clothes and sat down again. He asked, "Do you understand what I have just done for you? [13] You call me 'Teacher' and 'Lord,' and you are right, because that is what I am. [14] If I, your Lord and Teacher, have washed your feet, you also should wash each other's feet. [15] I did this as an example so that you should do as I have done for you."

John 13:5-15

4. List some simple, practical ways Christians can serve one another.

_____

_____

_____

_____

_____

5. In what circumstances is it more difficult to serve rather than to be served? Why?

_____

_____

_____

_____

_____

6. When is it more difficult to be served than to serve? Why?

_____

_____

_____

_____

_____

More from the Word

[12] God has chosen you and made you his holy people. He loves you. So always do these things: Show mercy to others, be kind, humble, gentle, and patient. [13] Get along with each other, and forgive each other. If someone does wrong to you, forgive that person because the Lord forgave you. [14] Do all these things; but most important, love each other. Love is what holds you all together in perfect unity. [15] Let the peace that Christ gives control your thinking, because you were all called together in one body to have peace. Always be thankful. [16] Let the teaching of Christ live in you richly. Use all wisdom to teach and instruct each other by singing psalms, hymns, and spiritual songs with thankfulness in your hearts to

God. [17] Everything you do or say should be done to obey Jesus your Lord. And in all you do, give thanks to God the Father through Jesus.

Colossians 3:12-17

7. What does it mean to be God's holy people?

_____

_____

_____

_____

8. If we have experienced God's unconditional love and forgiveness, what keeps us from extending the same love and forgiveness to others?

_____

_____

_____

_____

_____

9. How would our communities be different if everything we said and did was in obedience to Jesus?

_____

_____

_____

_____

My Reflections

"Are any relationships in your world thirsty for mercy? Are there any sitting around your table who need to be assured of your grace? Jesus made sure his disciples had no reason to doubt his love. Why don't you do the same?"—Max

Journal

Who is one person who needs to be reassured of my love and loyalty? How can I provide this?

_____

_____

_____

_____

_____

_____

_____

_____

_____

_____

_____

_____

For Further Study

To learn more about loving others, read 1 Corinthians 13:1-13; Ephesians 4:29-32; 1 John 1:7.

Additional Questions

10. How does it feel to be loved unconditionally? How does God's unconditional love alter our lives?

_____

_____

_____

_____

_____

11. How does withholding forgiveness from others affect us?

_____

_____

_____

_____

12. Explain the ramifications of the statement, "Forgive and you will be forgiven."

_____

_____

_____

_____

_____

_____

Additional Thoughts

_____ 19

_____

_____

_____

_____

_____

_____

_____

_____

_____

_____

_____

Extending God's Hand

"Jesus touched the untouchables of the world. Will you do the same?"—Max Lucado

1. Who are some of the untouchables of our world?

_____

_____

_____

_____

_____

_____

_____

_____

A Moment with Max

Max shares these insights with us in his book *Just Like Jesus.*

The banishing of a leper seems harsh, unnecessary. The Ancient East hasn't been the only culture to isolate their wounded, however. We may not build colonies or cover our mouths in their presence, but we certainly build walls and duck our eyes. And a person needn't have leprosy to feel quarantined. . . .

The divorced know this feeling. So do the handicapped. The unemployed have felt it, as have the less educated. Some shun unmarried moms. We keep our distance from the depressed and avoid the terminally ill. We have neighborhoods for immigrants, convalescent homes for the elderly, schools for the simple, centers for the addicted, and prisons for the criminals.

The rest simply try to get away from it all. Only God knows how many . . . are in voluntary exile—individuals living quiet, lonely lives infected by their fear of rejection and their memories of the last time they tried. They choose not to be touched at all rather than risk being hurt again.

2. What are some of the risks in reaching out to people with problems or special needs?

_____

_____

_____

_____

3. What kinds of things prevent us from showing compassion to others?

_____

_____

_____

_____

A Message from the Word

[4] But God's mercy is great, and he loved us very much. [5] Though we were spiritually dead because of the things we did against God, he gave us new life with Christ. You have been saved by God's grace. [6] And he raised us up with Christ and gave us a seat with him in the heavens. He did this for those in Christ Jesus [7] so that for all future time he could show the very great riches of his grace by being kind to us in Christ Jesus. [8] I mean that you have been saved by grace through believing. You did not save yourselves; it was a gift from God. [9] It was not the result of your own efforts, so you cannot brag about it. [10] God has made us what we are. In Christ Jesus, God made us to do good works, which God planned in advance for us to live our lives doing.

Ephesians 2:4-10

4. Describe how your new life in Christ is different from your life before you accepted him.

_____

_____

_____

_____

_____

5. What does it mean to you to know that you are saved by God's grace rather than your own good deeds?

_____

_____

_____

_____

_____

6. How have you benefited from the good works of others recently?

_____

_____

_____

_____

More from the Word

³⁴ "Then the King will say to the people on his right, 'Come, my Father has given you his blessing. Receive the kingdom God has prepared for you since the world was made. ³⁵ I was hungry, and you gave me food. I was thirsty, and you gave me something to drink. I was alone and away from home, and you invited me into your house. ³⁶ I was without clothes, and you gave me something to wear. I was sick, and you cared for me. I was in prison, and you visited me.'

³⁷ "Then the good people will answer, 'Lord, when did we see you hungry and give you food, or thirsty and give you something to drink? ³⁸ When did we see you alone and away from home and invite you into our house? When did we see you without clothes and give you something to wear? ³⁹ When did we see you sick or in prison and care for you?'

⁴⁰ "Then the King will answer, 'I tell you the truth, anything you did for even the least of my people here, you also did for me.' "

Matthew 25:34-40

7. What responsibility do you feel Christians have to help strangers in need?

_____

_____

_____

_____

_____

8. What obstacles keep us from helping the needy people around us?

_____

_____

_____

_____

9. How can we help others in ways that empower them instead of creating an unhealthy dependence?

_____

_____

_____

_____

My Reflections

"Oh, the power of a godly touch. Haven't you known it? The doctor who treated you, or the teacher who dried your tears? Was there a hand holding yours at a funeral? Another on your shoulder during a trial? A handshake of welcome at a new job? A pastoral prayer for healing? Haven't we known the power of a godly touch?

"Can't we offer the same?"—Max

Journal

In what tangible way could I help one needy person this week?

For Further Study

To learn more about helping others, read Mark 10:44–45; Romans 12:6–11; 1 Corinthians 12:28; Galatians 5:13; 1 Peter 4:10.

Additional Questions

10. What kinds of fears keep some people from helping others?

_____

_____

_____

_____

_____

11. What sacrifices do we have to make to show compassion?

_____

_____

_____

_____

_____

12. Describe a time when someone has shown compassion to you. How did you feel?

_____

_____

_____

_____

_____

_____

Additional Thoughts

_____ 29

_____

_____

_____

_____

_____

_____

_____

_____

_____

_____

Hearing God's Music

"Let God have you, and let God love you—and don't be surprised if your heart begins to hear music you've never heard and your feet learn to dance as never before."—Max Lucado

31

1. Describe a time when you felt God's presence.

_____

_____

_____

_____

_____

_____

_____

_____

A Moment with Max

Max shares these insights with us in his book *Just Like Jesus*.

In one of his parables Jesus compared our ears to soil. He told about a farmer who scattered seed (symbolic of the Word) in four different types of ground (symbolic of our ears). Some of our ears are like a hard road—unreceptive to the seed. Others have ears like rocky soil—we hear the Word but don't allow it to take root. Still others have ears akin to a weed patch—too overgrown, too thorny, with too much competition for the seed to have a chance. And then there are some who have ears that hear: well tilled, discriminate, and ready to hear God's voice.

Please note that in all four cases the seed is the same seed. The sower is the same sower. What's different is not the message of the messenger—it's the listener. And if the ratio in the story is significant, three-fourths of the world isn't listening to God's voice. Whether the cause be hard hearts, shallow lives, or anxious minds, 75 percent of us are missing the message.

It's not that we don't have ears; it's that we don't use them.

2. What is the difference between hearing and truly listening?

32

_____

_____

_____

_____

3. List some things that interfere with our ability to listen to God.

_____

_____

_____

_____

A Message from the Word

³ Then Jesus used stories to teach them many things. He said: "A farmer went out to plant his seed. ⁴ While he was planting, some seed fell by the road, and the birds came and ate it all up. ⁵ Some seed fell on rocky ground, where there wasn't much dirt. That seed grew very fast, because the ground was not deep. ⁶ But when the sun rose, the plants dried up, because they did not have deep roots. ⁷ Some other seed fell among thorny weeds, which grew and choked the good plants. ⁸ Some other seed fell on good ground where it grew and produced a crop. Some plants made a hundred times more, some made sixty times more, and some made thirty times more. ⁹ You people who can hear me, listen."

Matthew 13:3-9

¹⁸ "So listen to the meaning of that story about the farmer. ¹⁹ What is the seed that fell by the road? That seed is like the person who hears the message about the kingdom but does not understand it. The Evil One comes and takes away what was planted in that person's heart. ²⁰ And what is the seed that fell on rocky ground? That seed is like the person who hears the teaching and quickly accepts it with joy. ²¹ But he does not let the teaching go deep into his life, so he keeps it only a short time. When trouble or persecution comes because of the teaching he accepted, he quickly gives up. ²² And what is the seed that fell among the thorny weeds? That seed is like the person who hears the teaching but lets worries about this life and the temptation of wealth stop that teaching from growing. So the teaching does not produce fruit in that person's life. ²³ But what is the seed that fell on the good ground? That seed is like the person who hears the teaching and understands it. That person grows and produces fruit, sometimes a hundred times more, sometimes sixty times more, and sometimes thirty times more."

Matthew 13:18-23

33

4. How can we allow the teaching of God's Word to sink deeply into our hearts and lives?

_____

_____

_____

_____

_____

5. What things prevent some Christians from producing fruit?

_____

_____

_____

_____

6. Think of someone who is like the good soil, someone who hears God's Word and understands it. What characteristics enable him or her to do this?

_____

_____

_____

_____

More from the Word

²² Do what God's teaching says; when you only listen and do nothing, you are fooling yourselves. ²³ Those who hear God's teaching and do nothing are like people who look at themselves in a mirror. ²⁴ They see their faces and then go away and quickly forget what they looked like.

²⁵ But the truly happy people are those who carefully study God's perfect law that makes people free, and they continue to study it. They do not forget what they heard, but they obey what God's teaching says. Those who do this will be made happy.

James 1:22–25

7. Explain how we can hear something and agree with it but not let it affect our behavior.

_____

_____

_____

_____

8. How can self-deception lead to disobedience?

_____ 35

_____

_____

_____

9. What kinds of freedom or blessings come from doing what God tells us to do?

_____

_____

_____

_____

My Reflections

"Listening to God is a firsthand experience. When he asks for your attention, God doesn't want you to send a substitute; he wants you. He invites you to vacation in his splendor. He invites you to feel the touch of his hand. He invites you to feast at his table. He wants to spend time with you. And with a little training, your time with God can be the highlight of your day."—Max

Journal

What steps can I take today to improve the way I hear and respond to God's Word?

_____

_____

_____

_____

_____

_____

_____

_____

_____

_____

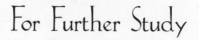

For Further Study

To learn more about listening to God, read Psalm 88:13; Psalm 141:2; Proverbs 2:1–5; Matthew 7:7; Mark 1:35; John 14:26; John 18:37; Philippians 4:9.

Additional Questions

10. In what ways does God communicate with us?

11. What places do you find most conducive to listening to God?

12. Describe the steps between hearing the truth and obeying the truth.

_____

_____

_____

_____

_____

_____

Additional Thoughts

_____

_____

_____

_____

_____

_____

_____

_____

_____

_____

_____

_____

Being Led by an Unseen Hand

"It's a wonderful day indeed when we stop working for God and begin working with God."
— *Max Lucado*

41

1. If your spiritual life was run like a corporation, what would your job description include?

_____

_____

_____

_____

_____

_____

_____

_____

A Moment with Max

Max shares these insights with us in his book *Just Like Jesus*.

For years I viewed God as a compassionate CEO and my role as a loyal sales representative. He had his office, and I had my territory. I could contact him as much as I wanted. He was always a phone or fax away. He encouraged me, rallied behind me, and supported me, but he didn't go with me. At least I didn't think he did. Then I read 2 Corinthians 6:1: We are "God's fellow workers" (NIV).

Fellow workers? Colaborers? God and I work together? Imagine the paradigm shift this truth creates. Rather than report to God, we work with God. Rather than check in with him and then leave, we check in with him and then follow. We are always in the presence of God. We never leave church. There is never a nonsacred moment! His presence never diminishes. Our awareness of his presence may falter, but the reality of his presence never changes.

2. What misconceptions do some people have about the kind of relationship God wants to have with us?

_____

_____

_____

_____

3. In what ways is God like a mentor to us?

_____

_____

_____

_____

_____

A Message from the Word

[5] "I am the vine, and you are the branches. If any remain in me and I remain in them, they produce much fruit. But without me they can do nothing. [6] If any do not remain in me, they are like a branch that is thrown away and then dies. People pick up dead branches, throw them into the fire, and burn them. [7] If you remain in me and follow my teachings, you can ask anything you want, and it will be given to you. [8] You should produce much fruit and show that you are my followers, which brings glory to my Father. [9] I loved you as the Father loved me. Now remain in my love. [10] I have obeyed my Father's commands, and I remain in his love. In the same way, if you obey my commands, you will remain in my love. [11] I have told you these things so that you can have the same joy I have and so that your joy will be the fullest possible joy.

John 15:5-11

4. How would you conclude the statement, "If Jesus is the vine and we are the branches, then . . . "?

_____ 43

_____

_____

_____

_____

5. In what practical ways can we remain in the love of Jesus?

_____

_____

_____

_____

_____

6. What kind of fruit would you like to bear?

_____

_____

_____

_____

_____

_____

More from the Word

44   ¹Lord, you have examined me
        and know all about me.
   ²You know when I sit down and when I get up.
        You know my thoughts before I think them.
   ³You know where I go and where I lie down.
        You know thoroughly everything I do.
   ⁴Lord, even before I say a word,
        you already know it.
   ⁵You are all around me—in front and in back—
        and have put your hand on me.
   ⁶Your knowledge is amazing to me;
        it is more than I can understand.
   ⁷Where can I go to get away from your Spirit?
        Where can I run from you?
   ⁸If I go up to the heavens, you are there.
        If I lie down in the grave, you are there.
   ⁹If I rise with the sun in the east
        and settle in the west beyond the sea,
   ¹⁰even there you would guide me.
        With your right hand you would hold me.

Psalm 139:1-10

7. What sometimes hinders us from experiencing and enjoying God's presence?

_____

_____

_____

_____

_____

8. Describe a time when you have experienced God's protective hand on your life.

_____

_____

_____ 45

_____

_____

9. How can we receive God's guidance?

_____

_____

_____

_____

_____

My Reflections

"People who live long lives together eventually begin to sound alike, to talk alike, even to think alike. As we walk with God, we take on his thoughts, his principles, his attitudes. We take on his heart." —Max

Journal

What does it mean to me to know that God is with me every moment and wants to play an active role in my daily life?

_____

_____

_____

_____

_____

_____

_____

_____

_____

_____

_____

For Further Study

To learn more about living in communion with God, read John 17:20-23; 1 Corinthians 6:19; Ephesians 6:18; Philippians 4:4-7; Colossians 4:2; 1 Thessalonians 5:17-18.

Additional Questions

10. What clouds our perception of God's view of us?

_____

_____

_____

_____

_____

11. What is the greatest comfort you draw from God's constant presence?

_____

_____

_____

_____

_____

_____

12. What responsibility does God's constant care put on us?

_____

_____

_____

_____

_____

Additional Thoughts

_____

_____

_____

_____

_____

_____

_____

_____

_____

_____

_____

Knowing Where to Look

"*Do you come to church with a worship-hungry heart? Our Savior did.*"*—Max Lucado*

51

1. Describe the hour before you arrive at your church for the worship service.

_____

_____

_____

_____

_____

_____

_____

A Moment with Max

God invites us to see his face so he can change ours. He uses our uncovered faces to display his glory. The transformation isn't easy. The sculptor of Mount Rushmore faced a lesser challenge than does God. But our Lord is up to the task. He loves to change the faces of his children. By his fingers, wrinkles of worry are rubbed away. Shadows of shame and doubt become portraits of grace and trust. He relaxes clenched jaws and smoothes furrowed brows. His touch can remove the bags of exhaustion from beneath the eyes and turn tears of despair into tears of peace.

How? Through worship. . . .

Worship is the act of magnifying God. Enlarging our vision of him. Stepping into the cockpit to see where he sits and observe how he works. Of course, his size doesn't change, but our perception of him does. As we draw nearer, he seems larger. Isn't that what we need? A big view of God? Don't we have big problems, big worries, big questions? Of course we do. Hence we need a big view of God.

52

2. In your own words, describe the purpose of worship.

_____

_____

_____

_____

3. In what kind of environment do you worship best?

_____

_____

_____

_____

A Message from the Word

¹I will praise the Lord at all times;
    his praise is always on my lips.
² My whole being praises the Lord.
    The poor will hear and be glad.
³ Glorify the Lord with me,
    and let us praise his name together.
⁴ I asked the Lord for help, and he answered me.
    He saved me from all that I feared.
⁵ Those who go to him for help are happy,
    and they are never disgraced.
⁶ This poor man called, and the Lord heard him
    and saved him from all his troubles.
⁷ The angel of the Lord camps around those who fear God,
    and he saves them.

Psalm 34:1-7

4. In what ways can worshiping God change our appearance?

_____

_____

_____

_____

5. What does emotion have to do with worship?

_____

_____

_____

_____

6. How does music help people worship God?

_____

_____

_____

_____

More from the Word

[8] Lord, there is no god like you
   and no works like yours.
[9] Lord, all the nations you have made
   will come and worship you.
      They will honor you.
[10] You are great and you do miracles.
      Only you are God.
[11] Lord, teach me what you want me to do,
   and I will live by your truth.
   Teach me to respect you completely.
[12] Lord, my God, I will praise you with all my heart,
      and I will honor your name forever.

Psalm 86:8-12

7. In what ways is God unlike any other person or thing we could worship?

_____

_____

_____

_____

8. Think of a moment when you have felt compelled to worship God. What prompted your worship?

_____

_____

_____

_____

_____

9. How has worship changed you?

_____

_____

_____

_____

_____

My Reflections

"God is in the business of changing the face of the world. . . . Our goal is simply to stand before God with a prepared and willing heart and then let God do his work.

"And he does. He wipes away the tears. He mops away the perspiration. He softens our furrowed brows. He touches our cheeks. He changes our faces as we worship."—Max

Journal

I worship God because . . .

_____

_____

_____

_____

_____

_____

_____

_____

_____

_____

_____

_____

_____

_____

_____

_____

For Further Study

To learn more about worship, read Exodus 34:29, 33–35; Psalm 95:1–7; Matthew 17:1–5; 1 Corinthians 14:24–25.

Additional Questions

10. What are the benefits of corporate worship?

_____

_____

_____

_____

_____

_____

11. How does private worship affect your spirit?

_____

_____

_____

_____

_____

_____

12. In what ways are our everyday actions acts of worship?

_____

_____

_____

_____

_____

_____

Additional Thoughts

_____

_____

_____

_____

_____

_____

_____

_____

_____

_____

_____

Fulfilling Your Destiny

"Wouldn't you love to look back on your life and know you had done what you were called to do?"
                              —Max Lucado

61

1. When you were a young child, what did you want to be when you grew up?

_____

_____

_____

_____

_____

_____

_____

A Moment with Max

Max shares these insights with us in his book *Just Like Jesus*.

The heart of Christ was relentlessly focused on one task. The day he left the carpentry shop of Nazareth he had one ultimate aim—the cross of Calvary. He was so focused that his final words were, "It is finished" (John 19:30).

How could Jesus say he was finished? There were still the hungry to feed, the sick to heal, the untaught to instruct, and the unloved to love. How could he say he was finished? Simple. He had completed his designated task. His commission was fulfilled. The painter could set aside his brush, the sculptor lay down his chisel, the writer put away his pen. The job was done.

Wouldn't you love to be able to say the same?

2. How can we discern God's "assignment" for us?

_____

_____

_____

_____

_____

3. Describe the freedom that comes from knowing and following God's plan for your life.

_____

_____

_____

_____

_____

A Message from the Word

[3] Because God has given me a special gift, I have something to say to everyone among you. Do not think you are better than you are. You must decide what you really are by the amount of faith God has given you. [4] Each one of us has a body with many parts, and these parts all have different uses. [5] In the same way, we are many, but in Christ we are all one body. Each one is a part of that body, and each part belongs to all the other parts. [6] We all have different gifts, each of which came because of the grace God gave us. The person who has the gift of prophecy should use that gift in agreement with the faith. [7] Anyone who has the gift of serving should serve. Anyone who has the gift of teaching should teach. [8] Whoever has the gift of encouraging others should encourage. Whoever has the gift of giving to others should give freely. Anyone who has the gift of being a leader should try hard when he leads. Whoever has the gift of showing mercy to others should do so with joy.

[9] Your love must be real. Hate what is evil, and hold on to what is good. [10] Love each other like brothers and sisters. Give each other more honor than you want for yourselves. [11] Do not be lazy but work hard, serving the Lord with all your heart. [12] Be joyful because you have hope. Be patient when trouble comes, and pray at all times. [13] Share with God's people who need help. Bring strangers in need into your homes.

Romans 12:3-13

4. Think of someone you know who is particularly gifted in one area. How is their giftedness obvious to you?

_____

_____

_____

_____

_____

_____

5. How closely do you think our gifts correlate with the things we passionately enjoy?

_____

_____

_____

_____

_____

6. How often do you think our call from God centers around our natural inclinations and dreams?

_____

_____

_____

_____

_____

More from the Word

⁶ And he raised us up with Christ and gave us a seat with him in the heavens. He did this for those in Christ Jesus ⁷ so that for all future time he could show the very great riches of his grace by being kind to us in Christ Jesus. ⁸ I mean that you have been saved by grace through believing. You did not save yourselves; it was a gift from God. ⁹ It was not the result of your own efforts, so you cannot brag about it. ¹⁰ God has made us what we are. In Christ Jesus, God made us to do good works, which God planned in advance for us to live our lives doing.

Ephesians 2:6-10

7. How should Christ's death on the cross affect the way we think about our talents and abilities?

_____

_____

_____

_____

_____

8. What gets in the way of us knowing and following God's call in our lives?

_____

_____

_____

_____

_____

9. In what ways has God prepared you to do the good work he has given you?

_____

_____

_____

_____

_____

My Reflections

"Regardless of what you don't know about your future, one thing is certain: You are intended to contribute to the good plan of God, to tell others about the God who loves them and longs to bring them home.

"But exactly how are you to contribute? What is your specific assignment?"—Max

Journal

What would I most love to accomplish for God?

_____

_____

_____

_____

_____

_____

_____

_____

_____

_____

_____

_____

_____

For Further Study

To learn more about the call of God, read Psalm 37:4; Psalm 139:15–16; Romans 8:28; Romans 12:3; Ephesians 1:17–21; 1 Peter 4:2; 2 Peter 3:9.

Additional Questions

10. What things keep us from discovering our giftedness?

_____

_____

_____

_____

_____

_____

11. Why do we sometimes feel useless if God has prepared us to do his good work?

_____

_____

_____

_____

_____

12. List several basic tasks that God calls all Christians to do, regardless of their gifts or abilities.

_____

_____

_____

_____

_____

Additional Thoughts

_____

_____

_____

_____

_____

_____

_____

_____

_____

_____

_____

Living the Truth

"The plain fact is we don't like the truth. Our credo is: 'You shall know the truth, and the truth shall make you squirm.' Our dislike for the truth began at the age of three when mom ... asked, 'Did you hit your little brother?' We knew then and there that honesty had its consequences."

—Max Lucado

1. What tactics do people use to avoid the truth about themselves?

_____

_____

_____

_____

_____

_____

A Moment with Max

Max shares these insights with us in his book *Just Like Jesus*.

The truth, we learn early, is not fun. We don't like the truth.

Not only do we not like the truth, we don't trust the truth. If we are brutally honest (which is advisable in a discussion on honesty), we'd have to admit that the truth seems inadequate to do what we need done.

We want our bosses to like us, so we flatter. We call it polishing the apple. God calls it a lie.

We want people to admire us, so we exaggerate. We call it stretching the truth. God calls it a lie.

We want people to respect us, so we live in houses we can't afford and charge bills we can't pay. We call it the American way. God calls it living a lie.

2. How do most people respond to flattery?

_____

_____

_____

_____

3. How would you explain to a child the importance of truthfulness?

_____

_____

_____

_____

_____

72

A Message from the Word

[22] You were taught to leave your old self—to stop living the evil way you lived before. That old self becomes worse, because people are fooled by the evil things they want to do. [23] But you were taught to be made new in your hearts, [24] to become a new person. That new person is made to be like God—made to be truly good and holy.

[25] So you must stop telling lies. Tell each other the truth, because we all belong to each other in the same body.

Ephesians 4:22-25

4. How do people usually respond when they get caught in a lie?

_____

_____

_____

_____ 73

_____

_____

5. Explain to what extent we should be truthful with one another.

_____

_____

_____

_____

_____

_____

6. List some dynamics that keep us from being brutally honest with ourselves and others.

_____

_____

_____

_____

_____

_____

More from the Word

[19] Truth will continue forever,
     but lies are only for a moment.

Proverbs 12:19

[22] The Lord hates those who tell lies
     but is pleased with those who keep their promises.

Proverbs 12:22

[23] Learn the truth and never reject it.
     Get wisdom, self-control, and understanding.

Proverbs 23:23

[26] An honest answer is as pleasing
     as a kiss on the lips.

Proverbs 24:26

7. In what practical ways can we seek the truth?

_____

_____

_____

_____

_____

8. How can honesty keep us from getting ahead in our professional lives?

_____

_____

_____

_____ 75

_____

9. Describe how important it is to you that the significant people in your life are truthful with you, even when it hurts.

_____

_____

_____

_____

_____

_____

My Reflections

"Do you tell the truth ... always? If not, start today. Don't wait until tomorrow. The ripple of today's lie is tomorrow's wave and next year's flood. Start today. Be just like Jesus. Tell the truth, the whole truth, and nothing but the truth."—Max

Journal

These are the truths that I need the courage to tell ....

For Further Study

To learn more about honesty, read Psalm 5:6; Psalm 101:6–7; Proverbs 12:22; Hebrews 6:18.

Additional Questions

10. Think of the most reliable and honest person you know. How do you feel when you are with that person?

_____

_____

_____

_____

_____

11. What price do we have to pay sometimes for our honesty?

_____

_____

_____

_____

_____

_____

12. How does it change a relationship when you suspect someone is being dishonest with you?

_____

_____

_____

_____

_____

_____

Additional Thoughts

_____

_____

_____

_____

_____

_____

_____

_____

_____

_____

Tending Your Garden

"The more selective you are about seeds, the more delighted you will be with the crop."
—*Max Lucado*

81

1. Think of one of the happiest moments in your life. What contributed to your positive state of mind?

_____

_____

_____

_____

_____

_____

_____

A Moment with Max

Max shares these insights with us in his book *Just Like Jesus*.

Consider for a moment your thoughts as seed. Some thoughts become flowers. Others become weeds. Sow seeds of hope and enjoy optimism. Sow seeds of doubt and expect insecurity. "People harvest only what they plant" (Galatians 6:7).

The proof is everywhere you look. Ever wonder why some people have the Teflon capacity to resist negativism and remain patient, optimistic, and forgiving? Could it be that they have diligently sown seeds of goodness and are enjoying the harvest?

Ever wonder why others have such a sour outlook? Such a gloomy attitude? You would, too, if your heart were a greenhouse of weeds and thorns....

If the heart is a greenhouse and our thoughts are seeds, shouldn't we be careful about what we sow? Shouldn't we be selective about the seeds we allow to come into the greenhouse? Shouldn't there be a sentry at the door? Isn't guarding the heart a strategic task?

2. List the three biggest factors that influence your thinking on a day-to-day basis.

_____

_____

_____

_____

3. What kinds of things immediately put you in a negative frame of mind?

_____

_____

_____

_____

A Message from the Word

23 Be careful what you think,
   because your thoughts run your life.
24 Don't use your mouth to tell lies;
   don't ever say things that are not true.
25 Keep your eyes focused on what is right,
   and look straight ahead to what is good.
26 Be careful what you do,
   and always do what is right.
27 Don't turn off the road of goodness;
   keep away from evil paths.

Proverbs 4:23-27

4. On a scale of one to ten (one being the least and ten being the most), how much choice do you think we have in our attitudes from one moment to the next?

_____

_____

_____

_____

_____

5. What concrete steps can we take to improve our attitudes about life?

_____

_____

_____

_____

_____

6. How does God's Word help us control our thoughts and attitudes?

_____

_____

_____

_____

_____

More from the Word

84

[7] Do not be fooled: You cannot cheat God. People harvest only what they plant. [8] If they plant to satisfy their sinful selves, their sinful selves will bring them ruin. But if they plant to please the Spirit, they will receive eternal life from the Spirit. [9] We must not become tired of doing good. We will receive our harvest of eternal life at the right time if we do not give up. [10] When we have the opportunity to help anyone, we should do it. But we should give special attention to those who are in the family of believers.

Galatians 6:7-10

7. In what ways can we invest in our own lives?

_____

_____

_____

_____

_____

_____

8. How do we receive returns on those investments?

_____

_____

_____

_____

_____

_____

9. To what extent do you think God holds us responsible for attitudes and thoughts?

_____

_____

_____

_____

_____

My Reflections

"Your heart is a fertile greenhouse ready to produce good fruit. Your mind is the doorway to your heart—the strategic place where you determine which seeds are sown and which seeds are discarded. The Holy Spirit is ready to help you guard your heart. He stands with you on the threshold."—Max

Journal

What areas of my life do I need to tend? How?

_____

_____

_____

_____

_____

_____

_____

_____

_____

_____

_____

_____

_____

_____

_____

_____

For Further Study

To learn more about guarding our minds and hearts, read 2 Corinthians 10:4–5; Philippians 2:1–5; Philippians 4:4–9; 1 Peter 5:6–9.

Additional Questions

10. In what ways does our society pressure us to please ourselves instead of God?

_____

_____

_____

_____

_____

11. How can we guard against the temptation to gratify our sinful desires?

_____

_____

_____

_____

_____

_____

12. What seeds of goodness can you sow in your own life or in the lives of others this week?

_____

_____

_____

_____

_____

Additional Thoughts

_____

_____

_____

_____

_____

_____

_____

_____

_____

_____

_____

Finding Treasure in the Trash

"How we look at life determines how we live life.... Here is what Christ did. He found good in the bad."—Max Lucado

1. Describe the most optimistic person you know.

_____

_____

_____

_____

_____

_____

_____

_____

A Moment with Max

Max shares these insights with us in his book *Just Like Jesus*.

God never promises to remove us from our struggles. He does promise, however, to change the way we look at them. The apostle Paul dedicates a paragraph to listing trash bags: troubles, problems, sufferings, hunger, nakedness, danger, and violent death. These are the very dumpsters of difficulty we hope to escape. Paul, however, states their value. "In all these things we have full victory through God" (Romans 8:35-37). We'd prefer another preposition. We'd opt for "apart from all these things," or "away from all these things," or even, "without all these things." But Paul says, "in" all these things. The solution is not to avoid trouble but to change the way we see our troubles.

God can correct your vision.

2. Why do we try to avoid troubles if we know God uses them for good in our lives?

_____

_____

_____

_____

3. Describe a situation that you found difficult to endure at the time, but now you are glad you experienced.

_____

_____

_____

_____

_____

A Message from the Word

[18] There was no hope that Abraham would have children. But Abraham believed God and continued hoping, and so he became the father of many nations. As God told him, "Your descendants also will be too many to count." [19] Abraham was almost a hundred years old, much past the age for having children, and Sarah could not have children. Abraham thought about all this, but his faith in God did not become weak. [20] He never doubted that God would keep his promise, and he never stopped believing. He grew stronger in his faith and gave praise to God. [21] Abraham felt sure that God was able to do what he had promised.

Romans 4:18-21

4. What is the correlation between our level of faith and our level of hope?

_____

_____

_____

_____

_____

5. How can we learn to focus on the positive rather than the negative during trying times in our lives?

_____

_____

_____

_____

_____

6. What makes you believe that God will do what he has promised, even when life makes you feel otherwise?

_____

_____

_____

_____

_____

More from the Word

⁹ What I say is true, and you should fully accept it. ¹⁰ This is why we work and struggle: We hope in the living God who is the Savior of all people, especially of those who believe.

¹⁷ Command those who are rich with things of this world not to be proud. Tell them to hope in God, not in their uncertain riches. God richly gives us everything to enjoy.

1 Timothy 4:9-10; 6:17

7. List some things that people put their hope in during difficult times.

_____

_____

_____

_____

_____

_____

8. In what circumstance do you imagine it would be most difficult for you to maintain your hope in God?

_____

_____

_____

_____

_____

_____

9. To what degree do you believe a person's ability to hope depends on his or her personality?

_____

_____

_____

_____

_____

My Reflections

"If you follow the example of Christ, you will learn to see tough times differently. Remember, God loves you just the way you are, but he refuses to leave you that way. He wants you to have a hope-filled heart. . . just like Jesus. . . . Sure, Max, but Jesus was God. He could see the unseen. He had eyes for heaven and a vision for the supernatural. I can't see the way he saw.

"Not yet maybe, but don't underestimate God's power. He can change the way you look at life."—Max

Journal

How do I need to change my attitude toward a particular trial in my life?

_____

_____

_____

_____

_____

_____

_____

96 _____

_____

_____

_____

_____

_____

_____

_____

For Further Study

To learn more about hope, read Romans 12:12; 2 Corinthians 1:5–7; Ephesians 1:15–19; Colossians 1:22–23, 27; Hebrews 6:18–19; 1 Peter 1:3.

Additional Questions

10. How would you respond to someone who said, "Hope breeds disappointment"?

_____

_____

_____

_____

_____

11. In what ways can hopefulness, or the lack of it, become a habit?

_____

_____

_____

_____

_____

_____

12. How can you develop a habit of hopefulness?

_____

_____

_____

_____

_____

Additional Thoughts

_____

_____

_____

_____

_____

_____

_____

_____

_____

_____

_____

Knowing When to Celebrate

"*Our greatest actions on earth go largely unnoticed and unrecorded. Dare we think that God is paying attention?*"—*Max Lucado*

1. What kinds of things do you think are too small to deserve God's attention?

_____

_____

_____

_____

_____

_____

_____

A Moment with Max

Max shares these insights with us in his book *Just Like Jesus.*

According to Jesus our decisions have a thermostatic impact on the unseen world. Our actions on the keyboard of earth trigger hammers on the piano strings of heaven. Our obedience pulls the ropes which ring the bells in heaven's belfries. Let a child call and the ear of the Father inclines. Let a sister weep and tears begin to flow from above. Let a saint die and the gate is opened. And, most important, let a sinner repent, and every other activity ceases, and every heavenly being celebrates.

Remarkable, this response to our conversion. Heaven throws no party over our other achievements. When we graduate from school or open our business or have a baby, as far as we know, the celestial bubbly stays in the refrigerator. Why the big deal over conversion?

We don't always share such enthusiasm, do we? . . . We may be pleased—but exuberant? Do our chests burst with joy? Do we feel an urge to call out the band and cut the cake and have a party? When a soul is saved, the heart of Jesus becomes the night sky on the Fourth of July, radiant with explosions of cheer.

Can the same be said about us?

2. What hinders us from exuberantly celebrating when we hear of some-one entering God's kingdom?

_____

_____

_____

_____

_____

_____

3. List some of the things that change when a person accepts Jesus as Savior.

_____

_____

_____

_____

_____

A Message from the Word

[4] "Suppose one of you has a hundred sheep but loses one of them. Then he will leave the other ninety-nine sheep in the open field and go out and look for the lost sheep until he finds it. [5] And when he finds it, he happily puts it on his shoulders [6] and goes home. He calls to his friends and neighbors and says, 'Be happy with me because I found my lost sheep.' [7] In the same way, I tell you there is more joy in heaven over one sinner who changes his heart and life, than over ninety-nine good people who don't need to change.

[8] "Suppose a woman has ten silver coins, but loses one. She will light a lamp, sweep the house, and look carefully for the coin until she finds it. [9] And when she finds it, she will call her friends and neighbors and say, 'Be happy with me because I have found the coin that I lost.' [10] In the same way, there is joy in the presence of the angels of God when one sinner changes his heart and life."

Luke 15:4-10

4. Describe a time when you lost something you *really, really* needed.

_____

_____

_____

_____

_____

_____

5. How does it make you feel to know the extent to which God and all the inhabitants of heaven rejoice when one lost person is saved?

_____

_____

_____

_____

6. Describe how you would feel if you had the privilege of leading someone to the Lord.

_____

_____

_____

_____

_____

More from the Word

[11] Then Jesus said, "A man had two sons. [12] The younger son said to his father, 'Give me my share of the property.' So the father divided the property between his two sons. [13] Then the younger son gathered up all that was his and traveled far away to another country. There he wasted his money in foolish living. [14] After he had spent everything, a time came when there was no food anywhere in the country, and the son was poor and hungry. [15] So he got a job with one of the citizens there who sent the son into the fields to feed pigs. [16] The son was so hungry that he wanted to eat the pods the pigs were eating, but no one gave

him anything. ¹⁷ When he realized what he was doing, he thought, 'All of my father's servants have plenty of food. But I am here, almost dying with hunger. ¹⁸ I will leave and return to my father and say to him, "Father, I have sinned against God and have done wrong to you. ¹⁹ I am no longer worthy to be called your son, but let me be like one of your servants." ' ²⁰ So the son left and went to his father.

"While the son was still a long way off, his father saw him and felt sorry for his son. So the father ran to him and hugged and kissed him. ²¹ The son said, 'Father, I have sinned against God and have done wrong to you. I am no longer worthy to be called your son.' ²² But the father said to his servants, 'Hurry! Bring the best clothes and put them on him. Also, put a ring on his finger and sandals on his feet. ²³ And get our fat calf and kill it so we can have a feast and celebrate. ²⁴ My son was dead, but now he is alive again! He was lost, but now he is found!' So they began to celebrate."

Luke 15:11-24

7. Before we come to believe in Christ, how are we like a rebellious, lost son?

_____

_____

_____

_____

_____

_____

8. Describe how you would feel if your child returned after years of separation.

_____

_____

_____

_____

_____

_____

9. How would we live differently if we shared God's deep sense of joy when one person entered his kingdom?

_____

_____

_____

_____

_____

_____

My Reflections

"Why do Jesus and his angels rejoice over one repenting sinner? Can they see something we can't? Do they know something we don't? Absolutely. They know what heaven holds. They've seen the table, and they've heard the music, and they can't wait to see your face when you arrive. Better still, they can't wait to see you ....

"You will be God's magnum opus, his work of art. The angels will gasp. God's work will be completed. At last, you will have a heart like his."—Max

Journal

What do I have to celebrate?

_____

_____

_____

_____

_____

_____

_____

_____

_____ 107

_____

_____

_____

_____

_____

_____

_____

_____

_____

_____

For Further Study

To learn more about salvation, read John 3:16, 17; Romans 3:23; 5:9-10; 6:23; 8:28-29; 10:9-10.

Additional Questions

10. List some reasons why we fail to see God as a celebrator.

_____

_____

_____

_____

_____

11. What factors in our recent history could have caused us to fail to celebrate at someone's conversion?

_____

_____

_____

_____

_____

_____

12. How do you think it would help you to annually celebrate your spiritual birthday?

_____

_____

_____

_____

_____

Additional Thoughts

_____

_____

_____

_____

_____

_____

_____

_____

_____

_____

Finishing Strong

"You know as well as I, it's one thing to start something. It's something else entirely to complete it." —Max Lucado

111

1. Name one thing you have never finished but you would like to complete.

_____

_____

_____

_____

_____

_____

_____

A Moment with Max

Max shares these insights with us in his book *Just Like Jesus*.

The Christian's race is not a jog but rather a demanding and grueling, sometimes agonizing race. It takes a massive effort to finish strong.

Likely you've noticed that many don't? Surely you've observed there are many on the side of the trail? They used to be running. There was a time when they kept the pace. But then weariness set in. They didn't think the run would be this tough. Or they were discouraged by a bump and daunted by a fellow runner. Whatever the reason, they don't run anymore. They may be Christians. They may come to church. They may put a buck in the plate and warm a pew, but their hearts aren't in the race. They retired before their time. Unless something changes, their best work will have been their first work, and they will finish with a whimper.

By contrast, Jesus' best work was his final work, and his strongest step was his last step. Our Master is the classic example of one who endured. The writer of Hebrews goes on to say that Jesus "held on while wicked people were doing evil things to him" (12:3). The Bible says Jesus "held on," implying that Jesus could have "let go." The runner could have given up, sat down, gone home. He could have quit the race. But he didn't.

2. Describe a difficult test of endurance you have faced.

_____

_____

_____

_____

3. List three excuses people give for quitting when the going gets tough.

_____

_____

_____

_____

A Message from the Word

[1] We have around us many people whose lives tell us what faith means. So let us run the race that is before us and never give up. We should remove from our lives anything that would get in the way and the sin that so easily holds us back. [2] Let us look only to Jesus, the One who began our faith and who makes it perfect. He suffered death on the cross. But he accepted the shame as if it were nothing because of the joy that God put before him. And now he is sitting at the right side of God's throne. [3] Think about Jesus' example. He held on while wicked people were doing evil things to him. So do not get tired and stop trying.

[4] You are struggling against sin, but your struggles have not yet caused you to be killed. [5] You have forgotten the encouraging words that call you his children:

"My child, don't think the Lord's discipline is worth nothing,
　　and don't stop trying when he corrects you.
[6] The Lord disciplines those he loves,
　　and he punishes everyone he accepts as his child."

[7] So hold on through your sufferings, because they are like a father's discipline. God is treating you as children. All children are disciplined by their fathers.

Hebrews 12:1-7

4. How would you describe the difference between punishment and discipline?

_____

_____

_____

_____

_____

_____

5. How does God use hardships to teach us discipline?

_____

_____

_____

_____

_____

6. What is the correlation between discipline and endurance?

_____

_____

_____

_____

_____

More from the Word

¹ You then, Timothy, my child, be strong in the grace we have in Christ Jesus. ² You should teach people whom you can trust the things you and many others have heard me say. Then they will be able to teach others. ³ Share in the troubles we have like a good soldier of Christ Jesus. ⁴ A soldier wants to please the enlisting officer, so no one serving in the army wastes time with everyday matters. ⁵ Also an athlete who takes part in a contest must obey all the rules in order to win. ⁶ The farmer who works hard should be the first person to get some of the food that was grown. ⁷ Think about what I am saying, because the Lord will give you the ability to understand everything.

⁸ Remember Jesus Christ, who was raised from the dead, who is from

the family of David. This is the Good News I preach, [9] and I am suffering because of it to the point of being bound with chains like a criminal. But God's teaching is not in chains. [10] So I patiently accept all these troubles so that those whom God has chosen can have the salvation that is in Christ Jesus. With that salvation comes glory that never ends.

2 Timothy 2:1-10

7. List some ways being a Christian is like being a soldier.

_____

_____

_____

_____

8. What kinds of things did Christ endure during his short lifetime?

_____ *115*

_____

_____

_____

9. If we endure and stay true to our convictions, even when no one is looking, how is God's kingdom advanced?

_____

_____

_____

_____

My Reflections

"We'll take our places at the table. In an hour that has no end, we will rest. Surrounded by saints and engulfed by Jesus himself, the work will, indeed, be finished. The final harvest will have been gathered, we will be seated, and Christ will christen the meal with these words: 'Well done, good and faithful servant' (Matthew 25:23 KJV).

"And in that moment, the race will have been worth it."

Journal

How can I prepare for the challenges I face in my race this week?

_____

_____

_____

_____

_____

_____

_____

_____

_____

_____

_____

_____

_____

_____

For Further Study

To learn more about endurance, read Colossians 1:11-12; 1 Timothy 4:15-16; 2 Timothy 4:5; Hebrews 10:35-36; Revelation 2:2-3.

Additional Questions

10. How do you feel about the phrase "giving up"?

_____

_____

_____

_____

_____

11. In your own life, how do you know when to push yourself to keep going and when to give up?

_____

_____

_____

_____

_____

_____

12. Describe how your experience as a Christian has been like a race.

_____

_____

_____

_____

_____

_____

Additional Thoughts

_____

_____

_____

_____

_____

_____

_____

_____

_____

_____

_____